YOUR ST

*An illustrated guide book to
simple psychology and therapy*

YOUR STORY

An illustrated guide book to simple psychology and therapy

by Alison Warden

drawings by Ben Warden

ALBEN BOOKS

Published by Alben Books in 2012
First published as *Damage and Repair* in 2006

Alben Books
19 Frensham Road
Sweet Briar Industrial Estate
Norwich NR3 2BT

Printed in China

ISBN 978-0-9572512-0-5

To my mother's memory

*"The flower that blooms in adversity
is the most rare and beautiful of all"*
CHINESE LEGEND

Once upon a time, according to an old oriental fable, the gods created the World. Together they created the seas, the mountains, the sun, the moon and the stars. They made the flowers, the clouds, the trees and the animals. When the World was ready they created the Human Being. Then they created Truth. Where should they hide Truth so that the Human Being would not find it immediately? The gods wanted to make finding Truth the ultimate adventure.

"We should hide Truth on the farthest star," suggested one god.

"Let us conceal it at the very bottom of the deepest ocean," said another.

"Why not place it on the very top of the highest summit of the highest mountain?"

Eventually, the eldest and wisest of all the gods declared, "No. We will hide Truth in the heart of every Human Being. In this way, he will endeavour to search through out the World until the day he stops to hear the voice of Truth within."

nce upon a time, about three and a half billion years ago, a miracle happened. The miracle was given the name – life.

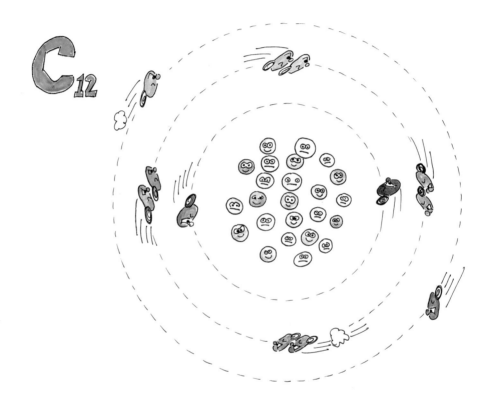

4

Nobody knows exactly how life was first created. It is known, however, that life is made up of small atoms, which are the smallest particles of a chemical element. Within each atom is a central nucleus. This nucleus is made up of protons, which carry a charge of positive energy and of neutrons, which have no charge at all. Orbiting around the nucleus, move electrons, which carry a negative charge of electricity. In a complete atom there is a balance of positive and negative electricity. All life is based upon the atom called carbon and all life is composed of energy. From the simplest life form to the most complex, all forms of life obey these same physical laws of nature.

Homosapien man is the most sophisticated form of life.
It is the complexities of his brain that gives him this advantage over all other living beings.

The Human Being is made up of a complex energy system. He stores energy from the food that he eats. He then uses this stored energy for different functions; for breathing, digesting, moving, thinking, remembering, circulating his blood and for simply being alive. These different functions use various forms of energy e.g. thermal, electrical, mechanical, chemical and psychic. Each has different and specific function.

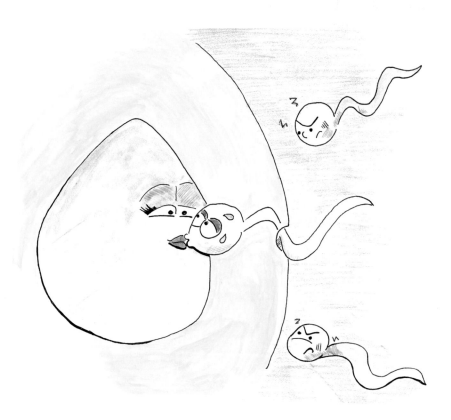

L ike all other animals and plants, the Human Being has a reproductive system. One male Human Being and one female Human Being, together, can recreate the miracle of life. During sexual intercourse, the male ejects between two hundred and five hundred million sperm into the female. It takes only one spermatozoon to fuse with the ovum in the uterine tube in the female. This union is called fertilization. In each egg cell and sperm cell is a nucleus. In the nucleus of each cell are many thousands of genes. Each gene is made up of deoxyribonucleic acid, which is generally referred to as D.N.A. In each double strand of D.N.A is stored the genetic blue print from each parent. It then processes exact copies of itself. By the time the fertilized egg reaches the uterus, it has divided five or six times and now consists of up to sixty-four replicas of its original self.

Three layers of cells form within the first week of the foetus being in the uterus. The outer layer of cells creates the nervous system, the skin, hair, nails and tooth enamel. The middle layer of cells form the bones, muscles, kidneys and circulatory system. The inner layer creates the respiratory system, digestive tract and the glands. The Human Being is a combination of all three layers of cells. However, sometimes one layer of cells grows faster than the others and certain characteristics can be observed. If the outer layer develops faster, then this Human Being will appear long in size and have a developed sense of intellect. This type of person is known as an ectomorph. If the Human Being seems muscular and adventurous, he would be termed as a mesomorph, because his middle layer developed faster. The digestive type is known as an endomorph with his inner layer of cells growing faster. He appears wide and obviously enjoys his food.

One single fertilized egg begins the miracle of life. Approximately nine months and six trillion cells later, it enters the world as a baby Human Being. In each of the six trillion cells is the infinite intelligence and wisdom of that first fertilized single cell.

There is no other living cell in the whole of the universe with that exact same blue print, (with the exception of identical twins), that shares this unique genetic information. This explains why each and every Human Being is totally individual.

All life, animals and plants, contain this innate organising power, this unparalleled wonder, the miracle of life. All of life, therefore, is interconnected which ultimately connects all living matter.

Biologically, the Human body is self- regulating. The wisdom of the body is always striving to maintain the fine balance of the opposing positive and negative forces within. Balance relies on opposites; hence the duality of all life. This self -regulation or healing is called homeostasis.

Energy flows through the physical body. When the energy is flowing freely the Human Being experiences physical wellbeing and good health. The body has its own consciousness or awareness and is programmed towards this regulation and self- healing. He may therefore, manifest an illness or disease if there is a blockage to this free flowing energy.

The Human Being is made up of four different consciousness'; the body consciousness, the emotional body, the mental consciousness and the spiritual body. The physical intelligence is therefore interconnected to the mental, emotional and spiritual consciousness and may be the only means of alerting the Human Being to one or other consciousness being out of sync. This can be a way to signal him to change perhaps diet or life style. It could also be a warning to heal a damaged psyche, which is synonymous to an unhealthy belief system.

14

P icture the brain of the Human Being divided into three parts. The upper and lower brain, then the upper part being further divided into the left and right hemisphere. The lower brain is the unconscious. It deals with the body's automatic functions, with emotions and instinctual behaviour. The upper part of the brain is the conscious brain, the thinking part of the Human Being.

The left side of the upper brain operates the logical, rational and reasoning activities, whilst the right side deals with creativity and imagery.

Think of the left-brain as the scientist and imagine the right brain as the artist. The lower brain represents primitive, instinctual man.

The brain, therefore, governs the conscious and unconscious bodily functions. His mind governs who he feels he is and affects and influences his body as one entity. Each and every thought is firstly transmitted in the brain through neurotransmitters, which are the brain chemicals. These brain chemicals send out different messages to the body's physiology depending on the different thoughts and varying moods. These in turn create either beneficial or detrimental consequences.

Each and every thought, conscious and unconscious, carries a charge of energy. This charge of energy can be either positive or negative and will then affect the life and health of the owner. Every single thought carries a charge of energy; now imagine this energy is sent out into the universe. These thoughts act like seeds for the future and are being sown now. The Human Being's inner life with its conscious and unconscious belief system will manifest in his or her outer life. When the Human Being becomes aware of his thoughts and begins to decipher which one is positive and negative, he also develops the awareness of choice. He can choose to focus on the positive simultaneously acknowledging and reassuring the negative.

The third consciousness, interacting within the other two is the emotional body. The seat of the emotional consciousness is said to be felt in the solar plexus, commonly known as the gut. The little messengers called peptide molecules are located in the gut and the lining of the stomach and interact with the brain chemicals, once again linking the mind and the body. The physical and mental bodies develop respectively according to age and within the confines of normal development, the emotional body, unless properly nurtured, can remain infantile and underdeveloped. So there may be an imbalance if all these different aspects are not equally developed.

There is a myriad of emotions available to the Human Being's experience: joy, sorrow, anger, happiness, pain, ecstasy, tenderness, love, hate, frustration, resentment, contempt, lust, pride, shame, passion, courage, vulnerability, jealousy, compassion, excitement, loss, fear, fulfilment, bitterness, loathing and so on. For every feeling that the Human Being experiences, there is an equal and opposite feeling waiting in the wings. Each feeling is composed of energy. Emotion means energy in motion. When the feeling is fully experienced and then released, so too can the energy discharge. However, some feelings may seem too much, too overwhelming for the Human Being to experience. When this happens the feelings are internalized, turned inward, repressed and ultimately stored in the unconscious. The charge of energy is also repressed and in time develops into tension, which is stored in the emotional and physiological bodies, which can cause certain signs and symptoms of distress and discomfort. If the tension then builds up, rather like a volcanic eruption, an outburst may alleviate the pent up feeling. On the other hand, the energy that is needed from the system to repress the feeling, can lead to depression. The Human Being's natural healthy flow of energy is used to keep down the repressed feeling. This, together with the charge of energy, will drain him of his life force.

When feelings are processed e.g. fully experienced and released, there follows a natural healthy flow of energy circulating around the body resulting in well being and vitality.

The fourth consciousness entwined with body, mind and emotions is the spiritual body, also referred to as the soul. Unlike the others that are more evident and tangible, the spiritual consciousness is invisible and intangible. It is said that the eyes are the mirror of the soul. By looking into the eyes of the Human Being it may be possible to be more aware of the inner essence of the person.

The mental body directs the rational and thinking processes, whilst the spirit or soul guides the Human Being's heart. When he listens to his intuition, it speaks to him through his heart. His heart is the doorway into a higher consciousness. This dimension is better accessed through daydreaming, hunches, ideas, creativity and imagination. His heart may close when he has been emotionally hurt. He may resist opening his heart, which by now is full of pain and shame. He may struggle to keep his heart closed. However, his soul always beckons and guides him to follow his true path in life, which always involves the opening of his heart. It takes courage to connect with his emotional pain and shame, but this has to be experienced if he wants to begin the healing process. Just by knowing that this part of him is in need of his own love and acceptance can help him take the first difficult and painful step on the journey to transformation. As he opens to each part of himself that feels unloved, and as he embraces and accepts himself exactly as he is, so he begins to open to the unconditional love of his soul. As he develops greater self-acceptance, so he can begin to live by his own truth. He may start to let go of needing other people's approval. At times, he may need to dig deep into his own resources of courage and discernment to maintain his belief in self. He will learn the difference between the voice of his fear and the voice of his heart. The voice of his soul speaks through his heart with unconditional love. When he begins to feel his pain and hurt, his heart will open to be healed. As his heart opens so his soul emerges.

Each of the intricacies of the four different interacting consciousnesses, when in harmony, creates health and vitality. If, on the other hand, one or more is not aligned, then illness, disease or some malfunction can develop. This is an opportunity, albeit an uncomfortable one, for the Human Being to change somehow. It is never by chance that he feels depressed, out of sorts, suffers with rheumatism, has high blood pressure, is fatigued or so on. He may choose pills and medication to become more comfortable and to alleviate his symptoms. He can also choose to become his own Sherlock Holmes and investigate what each of the four entwined consciousness is about. If the Human Being is unaware of his own inner self, he may need to attract his own attention to himself in sometimes quite dire and drastic ways. For example, if he has been brought up to believe that he must always strive and work hard, regardless of how he feels, perhaps to the extreme point of exhaustion, what may happen? Inner self somehow forces the body into submission. Only by the body being forced to stand still through whatever means, can he then become aware of the voice of his inner self. If his heart is closed, and full of pain and rage, perhaps his blood pressure may almost blow a gasket in an attempt to change him. Perhaps he was brought up in a household where it was necessary for him to stay strong, thus rejecting his own precious vulnerability. This rejected vulnerability may be forced to emerge through an illness. The illness will break his defence down in an attempt to heal this shameful hidden aspect of self. He may never have been allowed to vent his appropriate rage and hurt as a child and consequently store deep feelings of resentment together with his hurt and rage. These unrealized feelings also take their toll. As he begins to respect the wisdom and intelligence of the malaise so then can he begin to restore his natural health and vitality.

The strongest and most primary instinct in the Human Being is the will to survive. From the moment that all the sperms enter the vagina during sexual intercourse, this primal fight for life begins. The second that one sperm alone fuses with one ovum creates Human life and the will to survive is also conceived. During the ensuing nine months and when the baby is born, this is the most fundamental and predominant instinct. During normal pregnancy there is an innate bonding between mother and the unborn baby, which is an instinctual attachment. When the baby leaves the womb to make its entry into the world, this innate bonding helps the mother to protect and fend for the totally helpless and dependant baby. This relationship between mother and baby is the most profoundly deep relationship that the baby will ever experience. Mother acts as a template for all subsequent relationships and is therefore the most powerful. In a tender, loving relationship with mother, she can bestow upon him his basic trust and security. However, if for any reason, baby is deprived of this instinctual loving bond, which began at the moment of conception, he may suffer consequent damage in the core of his being at a cellular, organic level. Consequently, all future relationships with other people, society and the world in which he inhabits will reflect this profound pain.

The baby needs his mother to satisfy each and every normal and natural need that he experiences. All his needs must be met for him to feel completely satisfied. He needs to be fed, to be held and loved, to feel safe and secure, to be comfortable, warm and dry.

If the baby is blessed enough to have his needs fulfilled, he is allowed to develop at his own pace and feels loved and accepted for who he is at any given time. However, these demands may be ignored and the vulnerable, helpless baby may experience cold, discomfort, hunger, even perhaps feel abandoned. His need is for someone to hold him and love him to enable trust and security to develop. If nobody is there to comfort and love him, his feeling of abandonment could totally overwhelm him. His will to survive is still the strongest instinct and to enable the will to thrive he must disconnect himself from his own life-threatening pain. So, as he shuts off from his pain, so does he shut off from his basic, natural, healthy need of being loved. His original natural need is now buried in the unconscious together with it's natural companion, the charge of energy. The healthy need may no longer be conscious, but nevertheless from the realms of the unconscious it makes its way by an indirect route, in the form of sublimation otherwise known as neurosis.

Father too, plays a profoundly powerful role in baby's life, either by his physical presence or the lack of it. So, too, does the father's emotional maturity or deprivation influence and affect the well-being and normality of his child.

From the on-set of pregnancy, mother becomes the main character, as in a play, book or film. This role of main character becomes greatly enhanced when father learns to play best supporting role.

As the father is not physically attached to baby, nor is he able to breast-feed, it follows that theirs is the first possible relationship, which is based purely on spiritual love. Therefore father's template, be it enriched or impoverished, becomes another major role model for all subsequent relationships.

The cherished, secure infant feels loved for being who he is. The infant who feels unloved begins to respond and behave in a certain way in the hope of being loved. He stops being who he was born to be.

The degree of self-esteem that a child feels for himself determines his own self-worth. To become who he was destined to be and to realize his full potential, he must value his own intrinsic, inestimable uniqueness. This recognition of his own intrinsic, inestimable unique self is the second greatest gift that a parent can bestow upon its' child. The first greatest gift is the miracle of life itself. As there are many parents without this second gift, it is improbable, but not altogether impossible, that they can give to their children the recognition of self, which they may lack.

With awareness, the Human Being can begin the transformational process of accepting and loving himself exactly as he is. This means unconditionally embracing his totality. Any defences that he has learnt in order to survive need to be loved and accepted as wholly as the essence of self. He may need to experience profound pain; the deep pain of simply being Human begins the transformation of healing.

To begin to understand the Human Being it is necessary to know that only a fraction of him is conscious. This means that the vast majority of who he is lies in his unconscious. Imagine an iceberg. Nine tenths of the iceberg is submerged beneath the depths of the sea. Above the water only one tenth of the iceberg is visible, comparable to the consciousness of the Human Being.

According to Freud, the total personality of the Human Being is composed of three main systems; the id, the ego and the superego. Freud said that as all life is made up of energy, and that because energy cannot be destroyed, it must therefore be transmuted or changed into another form. If energy is repressed in one system, it must then show up in another, somewhere else in the personality.

Now imagine a house. Imagine building this house. First the foundations must be dug for the house to be built securely. When the foundations have been dug deep enough, imagine then a cellar. In the cellar lives id. Id is like a demanding, hugely energetic, instinctual, infantile child that never grows up. Id wants, always wants and wants NOW! The id is unconscious, dark as the cellar of the house, and is bound up in the biological needs of the Human Being. Id's main function is the pursuit of pleasure and the relief of pain. Id is an instinctual driving force that must have satisfaction, whether the desire for satisfaction is creative or destructive. It is upon id that the rest of the personality is built.

34

L iving on the ground floor, above id in the cellar, is ego. Ego takes care of the house, does the shopping, pays the bills and generally reasons and thinks things through. He must not deny the existence of id, but he keeps him in check, so that the Human Being is not just governed by instincts, but also develops into a clear thinking, reasoning and responsible person.

When the baby is born, he is only id. When the demands of id are satisfied immediately, so too is the tension or energy alongside the healthy need immediately discharged. However, the baby must learn gradually about the process of frustration. In normal development, so as to avoid the possible withdrawal of mother's love, and to avoid perhaps reprisal, disapproval or even punishment, baby may begin to suppress and frustrate instinctual id. Gradually id becomes more and more under the control of ego. In a stable, healthy home life, the young infant learns to control his id with his ego, without overly repressing or denying id. However, he may be forced to deeply repress id so as to survive bad parenting.

The third system is called the superego. Imagine that superego lives in the upstairs of this personality house. Superego is the judge, the conscious, and the internalization of omnipotent parental authority. Probably the child's first teachers of morality and ethics are his parents. They teach him what they think is right and wrong, good and bad, according to their own values and beliefs. In time, the child replaces the actual real parents authority for his own inner authoritative voice. The judgement sounds exactly the same and is on constant vigil. The superego is always processing how he should think, how he should act, what he should do and what he should not do. Superego judges his every thought and his every action. Imagine now superego living upstairs with two different faces. One face of the superego has the power to make ego feel full of love for himself, when he judges that he has behaved with virtuosity. With the other face, he has the ability to condemn himself with hatred and even loathing when he judges himself to have behaved badly.

If energy cannot be destroyed, only changed in form, what then happens to the energy in the repressed id? The id's opportunity to materialise arises when the Human Being sleeps. Young and old, Human Beings dream each night to enable the repair of the hurts and pains from the day's events. Dreams are essential to the good health of the Human Being. Each night the day's events and dramas are processed in dreams. As he sleeps, so too does the system called ego. So now, at last, is the time for instinctual driving force, id to have his satisfaction and fulfilment. Because id lives in the cellar (the unconscious) it has no means, without ego, of deciphering the imagery experienced whilst in the dream state. At last! Id can relieve itself of its tension and energy and fulfil its creative and destructive forces. However, superego is still on vigil, and without ego functioning, superego needs protection. Id must disguise his life and death wishes in many ingenious guises. In the morning, when once again, ego is functioning and operational, it remembers mostly snatches of what appeared to be abstract nonsense from the previous night's dream. The tension that was stored in the id is now relieved, superego is protected, and ego is left merely somewhat puzzled. If id has needed to be deeply repressed, then the full force of energy must be released during dream- time and the dream may turn into a nightmare. This can be a most terrifying ordeal for the dreamer, when in truth it may be a healthy attempt to restore harmony and balance in all systems of the personality.

During dream analysis, the dreamer is encouraged to experience the origin of his pain to help him resolve his life's agendas.

From the moment that the two original cells fused together to create the miracle of life, the blue print of the unique individual Human Being began its lifetime's work of instruction and organisation. This instruction and knowledge is totally complete in itself from the moment of conception. The innate assignment of any living cell is to realize fully what it was destined to become from the very beginning of its' creation. This is a biological fact known as adaptation. Jung, once a student of Freud, called this same process, when applied to the Human Being, individuation, meaning self-realization. The assignment for the self is wholeness and it is a life-long journey.

Jung said that the self was the core, the nucleus of the Human Being and that everything else unfolds from this most perfect source of being. Imagine now a daffodil bulb planted in the soil. The bulb represents the self. In time, the bulb grows shoots that will gradually force their way up through the confines of the earth and eventually bloom as the beautiful daffodil flower. Above the ground, only the flower of the daffodil is visible. It has developed and taken its instruction and knowledge from the blue print in the bulb, much like the consciousness of the ego the 'I' or 'me', taking its intelligence from the blue print of self.

Jung named the part of the ego's personality the persona. The origin is from the Greek word, meaning mask as worn by actors. It is the face that has emerged through the necessity of survival. If the true self has not been allowed to grow and develop, then the Human Being may have to sacrifice his true identity to gain his parent's acceptance and approval.

Who then hides behind the persona, the mask? In the darkness of the unconscious lurks the shadow. However vehemently denied and rejected, shadow persists its' existence. If persona portrays the acceptable personality traits of the Human Being, then shadow must be composed of the qualities and characteristics considered to be negative and even abhorrent. Far more comfortable and non threatening for the Human Being to project these unacceptable parts of himself onto another Human Being. He will then judge these qualities at a distance rather than learn to know and accept them as a part of who he is. His unconscious quest, however, is to become a whole and integrated person, to unite his conscious and unconscious. He may therefore need to attract exactly those people portraying his own supposed imperfections so as to enable him to look at himself more honestly. Once again, when the feelings, however difficult, shameful and uncomfortable are felt and fully experienced, the pent up energy can discharge. A new, true self, full of genuine, healthy power and vitality emerges from the integration of persona and shadow.

ach Human Being's realm of existence is unique to him. One person may live totally within his own inner world, whilst another experiences himself out there in the world, communicating and interacting with his fellow man. There is then a chasm of experience between them. What better way to integrate these two diametrically opposed Human Beings than to attract them to each other? Perhaps they become dear friends, or lovers, or are born into the same family. Their growing and development involves each polarized 'Being' reaching a more central point, thus becoming more like the other. One Human Being can learn to reach out from his inner world to relate to the other, whilst the other needs to develop his experience of his own resources in his inner existence.

There are many continued patterns of behaviour that are passed on from each generation. These patterns leave their mark in early childhood during impressionable years and become the child's inheritance. If the child is constantly affirmed and securely loved he can build his life upon a foundation of basic trust and security. However, if he does not feel seen and recognised for the precious 'Being' that he is, then his intrinsic self-worth and self-esteem will be damaged. Without this essential acceptance and love that each and every child naturally needs, he may suffer deprivation in the core of his 'Being' and even in his spirit. His belief system is reinforced with feelings of worthlessness and inadequacy. He may be unaware that this is his belief about himself. This damaged moulding of his personality perpetuates the tragic pattern of attracting more to itself. What he learns from his role models is repeated and therefore reinforced.

The child that is constantly criticised and abused actually deserves the right to feel his appropriate hatred, rage and pain. However, he is but a small vulnerable dependant child whose investment in making his so- called powerful parents right is paramount. The consequence of this action is naturally then to believe himself to be wrong or bad. He may invalidate his feelings of hate and pain and so grow up within fear and insecurity. His impulse may be to ingratiate himself, which derives from the unconscious drive to fulfil his natural basic primary need to be loved. He constantly seeks approval and may develop a radar- like antennae sensitive to the slightest hint of disapproval and critique.

J ust like a starving animal in search of a crumb or two of food so the young Human Being scavenges for substitutes for his authentic need. His unconscious hope is that someone, someday, may actually truly love him.

In this hopeless quest he learns to respond in much the same way as a performing animal. He is now sacrificing his true self in order to be patted on the head.

Not to be forgotten are his repressed, healthy appropriate feelings of hatred, anger and pain. When he represses the feelings, he uses energy from his life force to do so. The energy that it takes to hold or block the tension gradually takes its toll, even if the maladies may take their time to manifest. A first healthy impulse is for him to lash out at his abusers, however this may result in further abuse, so he may need to curb this impulse. The secondary impulse is to turn the feelings inwards, therefore back on to self. When he does this, he hurts only himself.

Once upon a time in Africa, a baby elephant was born. Sadly, this baby elephant was taken away from its mother and into captivity. The baby elephant was so frightened and distressed that he tried to run away as soon as he could. To prevent him from running away, his captors tied a rope around his leg and staked the rope into the ground. The elephant was a prisoner. Try as he might, the rope and stake held fast. So, he tried even harder, using all of his strength, struggling in an attempt to free himself. Still, the rope held fast. After days of struggling to free himself he gave up, defeated. He had learnt that his strength was no match for the power of the rope.

Gradually, the baby elephant grew into a fully sized adult elephant. Now, with his immense strength, the elephant could easily rip the rope and stake out of the ground and become free, if he chose. The struggle that had happened while he was young and helpless, with his mind so impressionable, resulted in his captors knowing they only had to leave the rope attached to his leg. The rope acted as a constant reminder to his unconscious that he was still weak and helpless. There was not even the need now to stake the rope into the ground, so indelibly imprinted was that early memory. The elephant was conditioned into giving up his power.

If the adult Human Being has an imprinted abused child in his memory and psyche, he may project this image of himself out into the world. He may then attract to himself the perfect bullying person to help him to become whole.

Imagine the Human Being who has 'Victim' written in invisible ink across his forehead. The bullies of this world will unconsciously gravitate towards him, much like moths to a candle. A bully may appear to be powerful, but is in fact forceful, not powerful. The forceful bully needs to be controlling and domineering to feel comfortable and secure. These two opposites, the bully and the victim, may well be attracted to each other to enable one another to develop their own characteristics, which as yet remain infantile and immature.

A strong- minded person having unconsciously repressed his sensitivity and vulnerability now projects this shadow onto another suitable candidate. He is using his strength as a mask, his persona as a defence. The shame that engulfs the unacceptable part of himself, is in truth crying out at the deepest organic level for love and acceptance.

Conversely, the sensitive, vulnerable Human Being who has not integrated his shadow will repress his own power and strength. The bully will intimidate him until his fragility is strengthened through assertiveness. Until he is confident, he will submit to the bully's demands. First and foremost he must learn to love and respect himself. Only then can others recognise and respect his empowerment of self.

Inside the outer Human Being hides an inner Human Being. Picture a nut. The outer shell is formed as a protection for the inner kernel. The inner kernel, however, is the most delicious part of the nut.

The outer shell of the Human Being develops as a very necessary defence. The inner kernel's very survival may depend upon the outer shell. The Human kernel began life as needy and vulnerable and deeply in need of protection. Depending upon the emotional maturity and love of his parents – or lack of it – will determine the strength and resistance of the outer defence. However, after a period of time, this outer shell may actually prohibit the deeper needs of the kernel ever being fulfilled. In every layer of defence is bound up stored energy. The first break-through of the defence may be very painful, together with an uncomfortable feeling of shame. Sometimes defence erodes slowly little by little, whilst at other times huge blocks of defence and resistance are demolished to reveal the authentic essence of true self. Only now can he begin to grow the seed of real power.

58

Some relationships are based on a struggle for power. Each Human Being involved in this unconscious game has to be 'right'. The consequence is interminable conflict with little hope of true intimacy.

Like knights in armour, these two people are highly defended. Their defence manifests through sheer force of will or some form of manipulation, overt or subtle. Either way is a no win situation. If one of them, however, can find the courage from within to share his feelings of fear, vulnerability and even shame, with his partner, then the dynamics have to change within the relationship. Now there is at last an opportunity for true intimacy. The maturation process has finally begun when true feelings, however difficult and uncomfortable are shared and most importantly – heard.

At an unconscious level it is the prototype relationships with mother and father, which are being transferred and played over and over again in these subsequent relationships.

As a baby or infant the Human Being may have been subjected to continuous critique or worse still suffered rejection and felt unwanted. This child will feel his pain deep down inside at an organic level, in a place within, which is beyond words. This feeling of the rejected, unloved self will profoundly influence the course of his life.

Imagine a desperately unhappy, unwanted child who reaches out in the vain hope of finding what is missing. He is searching for support, emotional comfort and love. Sadly he finds himself alone, perhaps even desperate. He experiences the desolation of being Human and separate. Tragically, what can happen to reinforce his shameful feelings of rejection is that he may feel that he is unlovable and not worthy of loving because nobody is there for him. The real turning point can only begin when he validates and honours his uncomfortable and painful feelings with no harsh judgement. This is the first step to healing. His second step is to learn to embrace his feelings and the third is to learn to love them. He has to find enough courage therefore, to experience fully the weight and depth of his pain and anger, simultaneously finding his love and compassion from within. The rejected self can now be transformed into the authentic, beautiful being that he was born to be.

Sometimes a 'clingy' relationship is valuable temporarily in the process of healing a damaged Human Being. He may need to stick to his partner like superglue to prevent separation. Alternatively, he may use his anger to control and dominate. Any healthy relationship is based on love, trust and respect and is therefore an inter dependant partnership. Conversely, the clingy relationship's foundation is built on fear, insecurity and co-dependence.

Each of the two damaged people will remain as though they are gagged and bound in this way until one or both of them feels ready to leave or develops enough to grow independently.

64

Visualise a bird. Picture it flying freely. Now imagine it being held tightly in a closed fist. Inevitably the bird will at first experience fear, and then may begin to feel suffocated. At the first opportunity the bird will surely fly away. If, on the other hand the fist is unclenched and open there is a very real risk of the bird obviously flying off, but nevertheless a chance too, that he may return. So it is with loved ones regardless of whether they are partners, friends or family. Holding onto them too tightly for the wrong reasons may result in them struggling for their freedom. Generosity and trust, however, which spring from real love, allow each Human Being to let go of their loved ones in order to give them their freedom. It is far more likely that they will choose to return.

The journey of self-discovery and maturation necessitates the venture into the darkness of pain and emptiness before the healing and repair can commence. Many people, however, prefer to avoid this uncomfortable process and choose instead to become addictive personalities. Any activity, which is an avoidance of self, can be substituted. The use of tobacco, drugs, alcohol, shopping, food, and sex are quite obvious ones, but even the hormone adrenaline can become an addiction, too. If the child grew up in an unhealthy environment of perhaps anxiety or even violence, then his adrenal glands would be constantly pumping out adrenaline preparing him for the 'fight or flight' syndrome. At a crucial moment of danger, this hormone is essential for the safety and survival of the Human Being. However, experienced at an ongoing daily level, his adrenal glands will be over activated and he therefore remains in a constant heightened state of agitation and anxiety. The rush of adrenalin with its burst of excitement may then become confused with the genuine excitement of just being alive. He may then reinforce his addiction to adrenalin with a dangerous life style because the alternative may feel too boring to contemplate. He may attempt to fulfil his primary need to be loved, with a constant stream of 'falling in love' relationships. Once again he avoids the hard, indigestible idea of working through the unpalatable.

F or any Human Being to begin the inner journey into self-discovery and self-awareness he needs to remember the three 'C's'.

1. Courage.
2. Commitment.
3. Compassion.

Courage because at times throughout his inner journey he will need to dig deeply into his inner resources of strength and resilience to carry on.

Commitment because the process takes a good deal of energy both in time and financial resources.

Compassion because he needs to feel this for himself as he breaks his defences down one by one to encounter his vulnerability.

This is not just some masochistic venture into pain, for there is always a light at the end of the tunnel. At the end is the beginning of love and healing. To enable the damaged Human Being to truly heal he has to become authentic. Together with the guidance and support of an emotionally mature adult he is allowed to fully experience the depth of his feelings. He can be directed to the source of his rage. He must experience fully each damaged part of himself. He must vent his rage, enter the depths of blackness and despair, cry, even howl for the sadness in his soul, before uncovering the vulnerable essence of self. The moment that he begins to accept how he honestly feels within, is the very moment that he begins to accept himself. As Carl Rogers, the acclaimed Gestalt Therapist says: -*"Only when I accept myself exactly as I am, only then can I change."*

Each tear that the Human Being sheds contains toxins from the body that are healing in themselves. Picture a wound. The nature of the wound is to heal itself. Providing that there is no infection and that the wound is clean, Mother Nature forms a scab over the vulnerable damage. In time the scab drops off when the wound is nicely healed. However, the wound may become infected and therefore festers. Antibodies collect into mucus to rid the body of the infection. So it is with the emotional wound of the psyche. It needs to be cleansed of its' resentment and negativity by delving and digging into the core. Many tears of rage and pain may flow, much like the septic matter, the pus of the physical wound. All his darkest feelings, once experienced and then released, begin to transform. The empty void transforms into a fullness of being; sadness becomes joy, anger transmutes into power. The Human Being ultimately may finally complete his healing with a release and forgiveness of his assailant. However, he may resist this inner work and the root of the wound will not miraculously disappear through denial or ignorance. This Human Being may be highly reactive in a most inappropriate manner. To the unsuspecting victim it would appear that the septic matter of the wound has just been spat out all over him.

P icture a street. Everyone in the street has personal baggage. They may have bags full of rage, bags full of sadness, bags full of insecurity and so on. Each week, each household sorts through some of these bags for the refuse collector to take away.

Now imagine one particular household. The occupants refuse to sort through any of their difficult issues. Their bags begin to accumulate in every room of the house, until it is overflowing with everybody's personal baggage. It proceeds to spill outside. One day someone comes to visit. Any body that visits must tread carefully over and around the many over spilling bags. The visitor may feel uncomfortable, tiptoeing on eggshells so as not to upset the householders. He may risk confrontation with his hosts, but is far wiser to refer them to professionals for counselling and therapy. The only acceptable feelings in this household will be phoney ones, which help cover up the deeper unhappy ones, which slide under the carpet, out of sight.

There may be cause for serious concern when the Human Being has been badly damaged and at the same time has little awareness of his plight. His festering wound needs very little provocation to explode onto any other person at any given time. This unaware Human Being is highly defended and can become hostile and even violent at the slightest provocation. He will store pent-up energy in the form of tension, which manifests in periodic explosions to relieve the system. These outbursts may endanger him and his family. The entire family is at risk and needs professional support. They may need to separate, temporarily or even permanently for their sanity and safety. Children born into this disturbing family unit become life's victims. Too much bottled up anger creates troubled behaviour, whilst too much fear creates shrinking violets. Neither is naturally healthy nor wholesome.

Once upon a time in the hidden depths of the jungle, nestled a village, which comprised of various families. A wise man periodically visited the village to impart his wisdom and to look after the spiritual needs of the tribe. One day on his rounds he knew instinctively that something was wrong. When questioned, a tribesman informed the wise man that four of their beloved children had recently been killed from the venomous bite of a cobra. The wise man was greatly troubled and set off further into the jungle in search of the troublemaker. The wise man looked after and loved the animals as well as the tribe's people, but he knew that he would have to heavily reprimand the cobra. The snake duly arrived, hung his head in shame and understood the wise man's concern for the children. Before the wise man left, the cobra promised faithfully that he would stop biting the children. The wise man, much relieved, returned to the village with this reassurance and a promise that he would return in a month. One month passed and as promised the wise man returned. He smiled knowingly when he counted the offspring, and once again set off in search of the cobra, this time, however, to thank him for keeping his word. He journeyed once again further into the jungle, and was puzzled when he could see no sign of the snake. The wise man called and called, but to no avail. At length he paused to sit down and rest. It was then that he saw the cobra. Curled up behind a small tree lay the snake. The wise man was horrified. The poor snake was bleeding profusely and was covered in cuts and bruises. "Mr Cobra, whatever happened to you?" Asked the wise man. In a very faint and weak voice the snake replied. "Well, oh, wise man, since you made me promise not to bite the children, they have greatly taken advantage of me. They have beaten me with sticks and stones and hurled me against trees and now I am suffering." The wise man took the cobra into his loving hands to heal him and said quietly and wisely "Oh, Mr Cobra, I did indeed ask you not to bite the children, but I never told you not to hiss.

The moral of the story demonstrates the world of difference between abusing power and asserting true power where it is necessary.

A Human Being may consider himself kindly when helping or looking after another person. His motives may be completely authentic and pure. Sometimes his behaviour, however well intentioned can result from projecting a denied part of himself onto the other person. Perhaps the Victim's pleading voice is irresistible, or the pathetic expression intolerable. Thus, the strong responsible Human Being becomes like the fish taking the bait. Like the captive fish he becomes well and truly hooked.

A certain triangle well known in transactional analysis epitomises this game that is being unconsciously played. In one corner of this wrestling triangular ring is the player known as the victim. In the second corner waits the rescuer, while the final contestant hovering patiently in the third corner is known as the persecutor.

The moment that 'Victim' plays his part e.g. manipulates, then 'Rescuer' immediately jumps in and takes the bait. However, the corners and positioning of this triangle have an uncomfortable habit of shoving each of these contestants from their starting positions into their opponent's places. Hence, the 'Rescuer' who could not resist the hook of the 'Victim', is moved to the position of the 'Persecutor' or perhaps back to the 'Victim's' corner. Each player is cleverly manoeuvred in a few swift moves.

This is really a boundary of self. If the Human Being can develop clear boundaries and empowers another person who appears fragile and vulnerable, this triangular game will stop. He must learn to use one of the tiniest but most powerful words in the English language. He must learn to say "no". The consequence of him resisting the bait can allow the 'Victim' to take responsibility for him self.

This is a story about a fisherman who sat in his boat fishing all day. He caught one fish after another. A young, very hungry boy watched him, drooling at the mouth whilst the fish were cooking and sizzling over the campfire. The fisherman was a kind man and seeing the young boy's distress cooked and shared one of his many fish with the boy. He thought of giving more of his catch to his new friend, but an image of his own hungry family also came into his mind. What was he to do? And then he knew. The next moment, the fisherman and the young boy were in the boat and it took just minutes for him to teach the boy how to put the hook on the line and to caste the line into the water. The young boy learnt in those few minutes not only to fish but also how to empower himself.

Each Human Being creates his own reality. The moment that he chooses to accept responsibility for his own life, he stops being a victim. His new awareness helps him to see how he attracts certain people and how he creates events, like an actor in a play. He may become fed-up with being type caste. His old belief system was that, perhaps, he was dealt a rotten hand of cards in life. He begins to understand that whatever he believes about himself is somehow manifested in his outer life. He can now begin each day in a new way, knowing that he can, as far as possible, take control of his own life. He has the right to change himself and his choices in his life. He has no right, however, to change other people. He may now choose to assert himself, which can then have a knock-on effect on the other people in his life. As he begins to respect himself, he inevitably changes the dynamics in each and every one of his relationships. Sometimes this transformational process proves to be somewhat uncomfortable for others. They can feel threatened and perhaps insecure. Even though he has no right to change another Human Being, the fact that he is maturing and developing himself will inadvertently affect others in a new healthy way.

He broadcasts his new sense of worth and esteem out into the world at a conscious and unconscious level. Other people respond accordingly. At times, his path may prove arduous. A pattern of behaviour, which no longer becomes him, has to be experienced intensely and repeatedly before he can let go of it and move forward. With each new awareness and insight he moves to a new level of conscious awareness.

Picture a vast school in the Universe. As each pupil completes his work in a particular classroom of awareness, so he is upgraded to the next level. However, just as with any promotional achievement he may well experience the work in this new classroom as hard, perhaps even feeling that he is starting again from the bottom. When he has mastered the lessons in this new classroom so it is time once again to raise his awareness to yet the next level. Each and every level of awareness and consciousness therefore brings new challenges and fulfilments.

Many people search for fulfilment and success outside of themselves in the outer world. While this is a healthy and natural expression of who they are, it cannot alone fill the depth of their being. True, deep fulfilment is dependent upon the relationship that each person has with himself, in his own inner world. Self will be the one and only person who will be with him for the duration of his life. His true happiness and peace is entirely dependent upon how he feels about who he is. It is the wise and courageous Human Being who decides to embark upon the journey of finding self, accepting and loving self, and finding true peace within.

To begin each day in a new way, he needs to ask himself:

1. What do I really want to do today?
2. How can I best enjoy today?
3. What would I do today if I really valued and respected myself?
4. What am I doing today that I do not enjoy?
5. What changes do I need to make in my life today to enable me to live my own truth?

To enable him to know himself requires commitment and discipline. Life in post-modern society is often stressful, pressured and busy. These components take the Human Being away from his first duty which is his relationship with himself. He needs to periodically stop to remind himself that he is a Human Being and not a Human Doing.

Meditation is a contemplative exercise for the mind, body and spirit. When the Human Being stills his body, his mind then has an opportunity to cease its' normal incessant mind chatter which in turn enables him to connect with his spirit.

Imagine living with a chatterbox. This chatterbox is likely to berate and scold. It is imperative to discipline this chattering mind to allow the quiet of the inner voice to be heard.

To meditate, he must ensure that he is in a comfortable position. With his spine erect and shoulders straight and relaxed he can focus on his breathing. He inhales. This in-breath is slow and full and is breathed right down into his abdomen. His hand can be placed on his abdomen to ensure that with each inhalation the abdomen is pushed out. With awareness he then exhales gently. Now, with the exhalation he pulls his abdomen in. This slow and deliberate breathing is both calming and relaxing to the body and mind. This is the foundation of all meditation. The next step is to breathe in the next inhalation to the count of four. Once mastered he can increase the exhalation slowly to the count of six, then eight. The inhalation remains breathing in to the count of four, so that finally the out breath is twice the duration as that of the in breath.

The breath connects the mind, body and spirit. Without the mind travelling into the future or dwelling on the past it can be freed of its' everyday thinking and worrying. Gradually it becomes possible for the Human Being to master the art of experiencing the here and now moment of living life.

Compare the mind to a wild horse. The horse needs firm handling, discipline and kindness. So it is with the mind. As the Human Being concentrates on his breathing, so the mind becomes more still and controlled. There are a few different states of consciousness. Now his body is relaxed, his mind tunes into a different vibration, which can induce a connection with all living matter. When he practises this method of conscious breathing, by closing his eyes, by ensuring that his physical body is motionless, he can begin to explore his inner, spiritual world. He maintains this discipline each day, either at the beginning and/or end of the day. Like the captain of a ship who learns to handle his vessel through dangerous waters, so the Human Being who meditates learns to captain his mind, keeping it on course and focused.

In time, by increasing the duration of meditation, the practise becomes a daily habit and therefore an integral part of his life. His concentration develops, his awareness increases, and his clarity is sharper, simply by making the time to sit still, to focus his mind, which allows him to listen to his inner truth.

As he meditates, he begins to tune into his deeper part of himself, the part known as the soul. His soul is wise and insightful and is always guiding and loving him. Little by little his defences break down as his heart begins to open. With each layer of defence that breaks down he may need to remind himself that in his pain and loneliness he is struggling to find the light and love of his precious soul. It may be that during the blackest times that he is nearest to that light. When he touches this divine part of himself he merges with the purity of love. Now he can love himself for being Human. Unconditional love heals the damaged psyche. All Human Beings who are alive or who have lived have each received the first gift on earth. The gift of life. It is the responsibility of each Human Being to cultivate the second gift on earth. The gift of loving that life.

Now imagine that this sensitive, vulnerable and damaged Human Being is……

YOU.

Bibliography

Moore P. *Fun to Know about mysteries of space*.
   Love and Malcomson Ltd 1979

Pearce E. *Anatomy and Physiology for Nurses*.
   Faber and Faber Ltd 1975

Janov A. *The Primal Scream*. Abacus 1973

Hall C.S. *A Primer of Freudian Psycholgy*.
   The World Publishing Company 1954

Choprea D. *Creating Health*. Grafton Books 1987

Stevens A. *On Jung*. Routledge 1990

Buzan T. *Make the Most of Your Mind*. Pan Books 1977

Lowen A. *Bioenergetics*. Penguin 1975

Siegel B.S. *Peace love and Healing*. Arrow 1990

Perarshall P. *Super Immunity*. Ballantine Books 1987